Food Comes From Farms

Miles Taylor

Do you know where the food
you eat comes from?
Most of the food
comes from farms.

milk

peanut butter

bread

apple

3

The bread is made from wheat.

Farmers grow wheat on farms.

The peanut butter is made from peanuts.

Farmers grow peanuts
on farms.

The milk comes from cows.

Farmers keep cows on farms.

The apple comes from an apple tree.

Farmers grow apple trees
on farms.

People need farms.
Most of the food
we eat comes
from farms.